WITHDRAWN
• No longer the property of the
Boston Public Library.
Sale of this material benefits the Library.

15

Triple H
Pro Wrestler
Hunter Hearst Helmsley

by Angie Peterson Kaelberer

Reading Consultant:
Dr. Robert Miller
Professor of Special Education
Minnesota State University, Mankato

CAPSTONE
HIGH-INTEREST
BOOKS

an imprint of Capstone Press
Mankato, Minnesota

Capstone High-Interest Books are published by Capstone Press
151 Good Counsel Drive, P.O. Box 669, Mankato, Minnesota 56002
www.capstonepress.com

Copyright © 2003 by Capstone Press. All rights reserved.
No part of this publication may be reproduced in whole or in part, or stored in a retrieval system, or transmitted in any form or by any means, electronic, mechanical, photocopying, recording, or otherwise, without written permission of the publisher. For information regarding permission, write to Capstone Press, 151 Good Counsel Drive, P.O. Box 669, Dept. R, Mankato, Minnesota 56002
Printed in the United States of America

Library of Congress Cataloging-in-Publication Data
Kaelberer, Angie Peterson.
     Triple H: pro wrestler Hunter Hearst Helmsley/by Angie Peterson Kaelberer.
     p. cm.—(Pro wrestlers)
     Includes bibliographical references (p. 45) and index.
     Summary: Traces the life and career of the professional wrestler known
as Triple H.
     ISBN 0-7368-1311-X (hardcover)
     1. Helmsley, Hunter Hearst—Juvenile literature. 2. Wrestlers—United
States—Biography—Juvenile literature. [1. Helmsley, Hunter Hearst. 2. Wrestlers.]
I. Title. II. Series.
GV1196.H45 K34 2003
796.812'092—dc21   2001007720

Editorial Credits

Karen Risch, product planning editor; Timothy Halldin, series designer;
     Gene Bentdahl, book designer; Jo Miller, photo researcher

Photo Credits

AP/Wide World Photos, 4
Dr. Michael Lano, cover (all), 15, 16, 18, 20, 23, 26, 31, 34, 37, 38
Geiger Kraig/CORBIS SYGMA, 28
George DeSota/Getty Images, 42
Jason Szenes/CORBIS, 7
Jim Bourg/Getty Images, 25
Kevin Winter/ImageDirect, 13
Rich Freeda/WWF Entertainment via Getty Images, 10, 32
Sue Coflin/Getty Images, 41

2 3 4 5 6 08 07 06 05 04

Capstone Press thanks Dr. Michael Lano, WReaLano@aol.com, for his assistance in the preparation of this book.

This book was not approved, licensed, prepared, or endorsed by any wrestling organization, including World Wrestling Entertainment, Inc. or World Championship Wrestling, or any member of such organizations.

Table of Contents

Chapter 1   A Champion Heel 5

Chapter 2   The Early Years 11

Chapter 3   The WWF 19

Chapter 4   World Champion 27

Chapter 5   Triple H Today.......................... 35

Features

Major Matches 9

Triple H's Hero................................. 15

Rival in the Ring 32

Career Highlights 43

Words to Know 44

To Learn More 45

Useful Addresses 46

Internet Sites 47

Index 48

A Champion Heel

On August 23, 1999, wrestling fans gathered at the Hilton Coliseum at Iowa State University in Ames, Iowa. The fans were there to see their favorite World Wrestling Federation (WWF) stars in action.

Wrestler Paul Levesque walked into the ring. He is known as Hunter Hearst Helmsley, or Triple H. Hunter was there to wrestle Mick Foley for the World Championship title. Foley wrestled as Mankind. The night before, Mankind had won the title during a Triple Threat match at SummerSlam in Minneapolis, Minnesota. Mankind had defeated Hunter and

On August 22, Mankind (right) defeated Hunter for the WWF World Championship in Minneapolis, Minnesota.

Steve Williams. Williams wrestles as "Stone Cold" Steve Austin.

Going for the Title

Shane McMahon was the special guest referee during the Iowa match. McMahon is the son of WWF owner Vince McMahon.

Hunter began punching Mankind before McMahon rang the bell. Mankind then knocked Hunter down into a corner. He covered Hunter for the pin. McMahon was arguing with another wrestler on the sidelines and did not see the pin.

Mankind then put a dirty sweat sock on his hand. Mankind called the sock "Mr. Socko." He tried to shove Mr. Socko down Hunter's throat. But he missed and shoved Mr. Socko into McMahon's mouth instead.

Hunter then tried to perform his signature move on Mankind. This move is called the Pedigree. Hunter holds his opponent face down. The opponent's head is between Hunter's legs. Hunter drops to his knees as he slams his opponent's head into the mat. But Mankind backdropped Hunter to the mat before he could finish the Pedigree.

Chyna often helped Hunter during his matches.

Wrestler Joanie Laurer ran into the ring to help Hunter. Laurer wrestled as Chyna. Mankind shoved Mr. Socko in Chyna's mouth and pushed her out of the ring.

Late in the match, Hunter backed Mankind into a corner. Mankind escaped and clotheslined Hunter over the top rope. Mankind followed him out of the ring.

McMahon grabbed a chair and hit Mankind on the back. Hunter then picked up a chair and hit Mankind on the head. McMahon rolled Mankind back into the ring. Hunter ran into the ring. He took Mankind down with a Pedigree. Hunter then flipped Mankind over and covered him for the pin. McMahon counted to three. Hunter was the new WWF World Champion.

About Hunter Hearst Helmsley

Hunter Hearst Helmsley is 6 feet, 4 inches (193 centimeters) tall and weighs 246 pounds (112 kilograms). He began wrestling in 1992 under the name Terra Ryzing. Later, he wrestled as Jean-Paul Levesque before joining the WWF in 1996 as Hunter Hearst Helmsley.

Wrestlers play a role during their matches. Some wrestlers are heroes. They are called "babyfaces" or "faces." Other wrestlers act mean to their opponents or to the fans. These wrestlers are known as "heels."

During most of his career, Hunter has been one of wrestling's most successful heels. He has won the WWF World Championship four times. In 2002, Hunter became the Undisputed Champion of pro wrestling.

Major Matches

October 21, 1996—Hunter defeats Marc Mero to win the WWF Intercontinental Championship.

June 8, 1997—Hunter defeats Mankind in the finals of the King of the Ring tournament.

August 23, 1999—Hunter defeats Mankind to win his first WWF World Championship.

September 26, 1999—Hunter wins his second World Championship in a match against Mankind, The Rock, the Big Show, Kane, and the British Bulldog.

January 3, 2000—Hunter defeats the Big Show to win his third World Championship.

May 21, 2000—Hunter defeats The Rock in an Iron Man match to win his fourth World Championship.

January 20, 2002—Hunter wins the Royal Rumble.

March 17, 2002—Hunter defeats Chris Jericho to become the Undisputed Champion of pro wrestling.

Chapter 2

The Early Years

Hunter was born July 27, 1969, in New Hampshire. His parents are Paul and Patricia Levesque. He has an older sister.

Hunter grew up in Nashua, New Hampshire. He became interested in professional wrestling at a young age. On Saturday mornings, he watched wrestling matches on TV. Hunter's father often took him to see wrestling matches.

Bodybuilding

At age 14, Hunter became interested in bodybuilding. Bodybuilders increase the size of their muscles by exercising, lifting weights,

Hunter became interested in wrestling at a young age.

and eating healthy foods. They often compete at bodybuilding shows.

Hunter began spending most of his time outside of school at a gym. He developed his muscles by lifting weights.

In 1987, Hunter graduated from Nashua High School. He got a job at a health club as a personal trainer. He worked with health club members on their exercise programs. He later became the club's manager. But Hunter had not lost interest in wrestling. He thought he might have the body and the athletic ability to be a pro wrestler.

A New Career

At a gym, Hunter met former WWF wrestler Ted Arcidi. Hunter told Arcidi about his goal of becoming a wrestler. Arcidi knew how hard a wrestler's life can be. He tried to talk Hunter out of his decision. But Hunter did not change his mind. Arcidi gave him the names of some people in the pro wrestling business. One of these names was Wladek "Walter" Kowalski.

Kowalski was a top wrestler in the 1950s and 1960s. In the late 1970s, he started a

Hunter developed his muscles by lifting weights.

training school for pro wrestlers in Malden,
Massachusetts. In 1991, Hunter became a
student at Kowalski's school.

Hunter worked hard at the wrestling school.
He often was the first student to arrive at the
gym and the last to leave.

Kowalski was impressed with Hunter's
skills. After only five months, Kowalski
told Hunter that he was ready to wrestle his

first match. Hunter competed in a small independent wrestling company called the IWF.

Terra Ryzing

Before Hunter could wrestle, he needed a wrestling name. Kowalski suggested Hunter call himself "Terra Ryzing."

Hunter wrestled his first match as Terra Ryzing in Burlington, Vermont. He lost that match. But he soon began winning. By summer 1992, he was the IWF Heavyweight Champion.

Hunter continued to wrestle for the IWF in 1993. Scouts from both the WWF and World Championship Wrestling (WCW) began to notice him. WCW was based in Atlanta, Georgia.

In 1994, Hunter went to Atlanta to try out for WCW. WCW officials were impressed with Hunter's skills. They offered him a two-year contract. Hunter asked for a one-year contract instead. He hoped to develop his speaking and wrestling abilities in WCW and then move to the WWF.

Triple H's Hero: Ric Flair

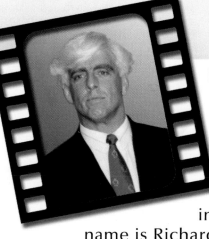

Hunter watched many pro wrestlers as he grew up. One of his favorite wrestlers was Ric Flair.

Flair was born in 1949. His real name is Richard Fliehr. Flair began wrestling in 1972 in the American Wrestling Alliance (AWA). He won several titles there before moving to the National Wrestling Alliance (NWA) in 1974.

In 1991, the NWA became part of WCW. Flair was the first WCW World Champion. Later in 1991, he joined the WWF. Flair won two WWF World Championships before going back to WCW in 1992. He became the WCW World Champion seven more times.

Flair wrestled for WCW until the company was sold to the WWF in 2001. Later that year, he joined the WWF.

Hunter wrestled as Jean-Paul Levesque in WCW.

WCW Career

Hunter joined WCW as Terra Ryzing. WCW officials soon came up with a new character for Hunter. He began wrestling as Jean-Paul Levesque.

The Jean-Paul Levesque character was a rich French-Canadian who thought he was better than the fans and other wrestlers. As part of the character, Hunter spoke with a French accent. He also formed a tag team with Darren Matthews. Matthews wrestled as Lord Steven Regal.

Hunter did not like working for WCW. WCW officials did not give him a chance to wrestle the company's top wrestlers or compete for a title. But Hunter was developing both his wrestling and speaking abilities. He thought he was ready for the WWF.

Joining the WWF

In 1995, Hunter called Vince McMahon. McMahon agreed to meet with Hunter. After the meeting, Hunter thought McMahon was not interested in hiring him.

Hunter went back to WCW. On December 27, he lost to Alex Wright at an event called Starrcade. Wright wrestled as Berlyn.

The next day, Hunter's mother called him at his hotel in Chicago, Illinois. WWF officials wanted to offer Hunter a job. Hunter's dream of being a WWF wrestler was about to come true.

Chapter 3

The WWF

In early 1996, Hunter joined the WWF as Hunter Hearst Helmsley. The character's personality was much like that of Jean-Paul Levesque. The character was from the wealthy town of Greenwich, Connecticut. He was called "the Greenwich Snob." Hunter also developed the Pedigree as his signature move.

Career Setback

Hunter quickly became close friends with several WWF wrestlers. These wrestlers were Kevin Nash, Scott Hall, Michael Hickenbottom, and Sean Waltman. At the time, Nash was known as Diesel. Hall wrestled

Hunter joined the WWF in 1996.

Shawn Michaels and Hunter became close friends after Hunter joined the WWF.

as Razor Ramon. Hickenbottom wrestled as Shawn Michaels. Waltman wrestled as X-Pac.

On May 19, 1996, the WWF had a show at Madison Square Garden in New York City. Hunter was scheduled to wrestle Hall. Michaels would wrestle Nash. The show would be the last WWF event for Hall and Nash. They were leaving the company to join WCW.

Hunter had defeated Hall earlier in the night. After Michaels defeated Nash, Hunter and Hall joined them in the ring. The four men hugged and gave each other high fives.

Outside the ring, wrestlers often are good friends with their rivals. But they do not show their feelings during matches.

Many people in the wrestling business did not like the group's actions. They wanted Vince McMahon to punish the two wrestlers who remained in the WWF. Michaels was the WWF World Champion and one of the most popular wrestlers in the company. McMahon did not want to punish him, but he could punish Hunter.

Hunter wrestled the next week on TV. After that, he did not appear on the WWF's TV shows for nearly six months. WWF officials did not allow him to compete in the King of the Ring tournament in June. Steve Austin took his place and won the tournament.

A Championship and a Bodyguard

On October 21, 1996, Hunter wrestled Marc Mero in Fort Wayne, Indiana. Mero was the Intercontinental Champion. During the match, wrestler Curt Hennig helped Hunter. Hennig wrestles as Mr. Perfect. He hit Mero with a chair. Hunter then gave Mero a Pedigree for the win. The championship was Hunter's first major wrestling title.

On February 13, 1997, Hunter lost the Intercontinental title to Dwayne Johnson. Johnson wrestles as The Rock. After this match, Chyna joined the WWF. During matches, she acted as Hunter's bodyguard. She sometimes ran into the ring to attack Hunter's opponent. Her actions usually allowed Hunter to win the match.

Hunter was a heel. Fans often booed him at matches. But they still enjoyed watching him wrestle.

On June 8, 1997, Hunter defeated Mankind to win the King of the Ring tournament. Hunter and Mankind continued their rivalry through the summer. On August 3, they met in a cage match at SummerSlam. Mankind

Hunter became the Intercontinental Champion in 1996.

defeated Hunter with an elbow drop off the top of the cage.

D-Generation X

In October 1997, Hunter teamed with Shawn Michaels and Chyna. They formed a group called D-Generation X (DX).

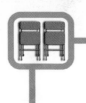

I've had a long, long run of just being hated by the fans. It hasn't been by accident. I want it that way.
—**Hunter Hearst Helmsley,**
***RAW* magazine, June 2001**

The DX members wrestled together. Between matches, they made fun of WWF officials and other wrestlers.

Hunter also changed his character's attitude and looks. He acted tough in the ring. He wore T-shirts, jeans, a leather cap, and sunglasses.

In December 1997, Hunter achieved another goal. Hunter became the European Champion when Shawn Michaels gave up the title.

Shawn Michaels was DX's leader. In March 1998, Michaels had to stop wrestling because of an injury. Hunter then took over as the leader. Other wrestlers also joined the group. These wrestlers were X-Pac, Monty Sopt, and Brian James. Sopt wrestles as Billy Gunn. James is Road Dogg.

Hunter continued to wrestle well. Many of his best matches were against The Rock. On August 30, 1998, Hunter wrestled The Rock in a ladder match at SummerSlam. At the time,

In 1998, boxer Mike Tyson joined DX in the ring at WrestleMania 14.

The Rock was the Intercontinental Champion. Hunter won the match and the title.

Hunter wrestled with DX off and on for nearly two years. During that time, fans began to cheer for the DX members. They became babyfaces. Hunter preferred being a heel. In March 1999, he left DX to wrestle on his own.

Chapter 4

World Champion

On August 22, 1999, Hunter got his first chance to wrestle for the WWF World Championship. He faced Steve Austin and Mankind at a Triple Threat match at SummerSlam. Mankind won the match. But Hunter came back the next night to defeat Mankind for the title.

On September 14, Vince McMahon challenged Hunter for the title. McMahon was not a wrestler. Steve Austin ran into the match to help McMahon pin Hunter and win the title. After the match, McMahon said he would give up the title at Unforgiven. This event was set for September 26 in Charlotte, North Carolina.

Hunter won his first WWF World Championship in 1999.

Hunter defended his title several times during 2000.

Six-Pack Match

At Unforgiven, Hunter faced five wrestlers for the World Championship. These wrestlers were Mankind, The Rock, Paul Wight, Glen Jacobs, and David Smith. Wight wrestles as the Big Show. Jacobs wrestles as Kane. Smith is known as the British Bulldog.

During the match, the six wrestlers battled both inside and outside of the ring. Late in the match, The Rock tried to pin Hunter. But the Bulldog ran in the ring and hit The Rock with a chair. Hunter took down The Rock with a Pedigree and covered him for the pin. Hunter was again the World Champion.

Hunter held the title until November 14, 1999. He wrestled The Rock and the Big Show in a Triple Threat match at Survivor Series in Detroit, Michigan. The Big Show defeated Hunter and The Rock to win the title.

A New Year

Hunter began 2000 by wrestling the Big Show on January 3 in Miami, Florida. Hunter won the match and the World Championship.

Hunter defended his title several times during the next few months. Mick Foley was his opponent during three of these matches.

Foley usually wrestled as Mankind. He had been known as Cactus Jack earlier in his career. On January 23, Foley wrestled as Cactus Jack during a street fight match with Hunter at Madison Square Garden. Hunter defeated Cactus Jack.

On February 27, Hunter wrestled Cactus Jack in a cage match. The wrestlers battled inside and outside of the steel cage. Both climbed to the top of the cage. Hunter picked up Cactus Jack and threw him down on the cage. Cactus Jack fell through the cage and the ring. Hunter then climbed into the cage. He gave Cactus Jack a Pedigree for the win.

On April 2, Hunter defended his title at WrestleMania 16 in Anaheim, California. Hunter's opponents were Mick Foley, The Rock, and the Big Show. Foley wrestled under his real name during this match.

Hunter first worked with The Rock and Foley to pin the Big Show. Hunter hit Foley with a chair and pinned him with the Pedigree. Hunter then pinned The Rock to win the match and keep the title.

Hunter and The Rock

Hunter held the World Champion title until April 30, 2000. That night, he wrestled The Rock at Backlash in Washington, D.C. The Rock defeated Hunter for the title.

During 2000, Hunter wrestled several great matches against The Rock.

On May 21, 2000, Hunter and The Rock met in an Iron Man Match for the World Championship. The match lasted one hour. The two wrestlers tried to pin each other as many times as they could.

Hunter and The Rock battled inside and outside of the ring. With 2 minutes left, they were tied with five pins each. X-Pac, Road Dogg, and Mark Callaway then entered the

Hunter has wrestled many matches against "Stone Cold" Steve Austin. They first faced each other October 20, 1996. Austin defeated Hunter in this match.

Austin was born in 1964 in Texas. His real name is Steve Williams. He is 6 feet, 2 inches (188 centimeters) tall and weighs 252 pounds (114 kilograms). His signature move is the Stone Cold Stunner.

Austin played football in college before beginning his wrestling career in 1989. He first wrestled for World Class Championship Wrestling (WCCW) in Texas. He also wrestled for WCW and Extreme Championship Wrestling (ECW). He joined the WWF in 1995.

Austin has won the WWF World Championship six times and the WWF Intercontinental Championship twice. He also is a four-time WWF Tag Team Champion. He teamed with Hunter to win one of his Tag Team titles.

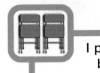

> I put my life on the line every day for our business, and I gladly do it, and I will continue to do it, until I can do it no longer.
> —Hunter Hearst Helmsley,
> MTV's *Tough Enough*, 7/5/01

ring. Callaway wrestles as the Undertaker. The Undertaker chokeslammed Hunter to the mat. The referee disqualified The Rock because of the Undertaker's action. Hunter won the match and the title.

A Challenge to the Title

In June, Hunter wrestled in a six-man tag team match at the King of the Ring tournament. He wrestled with Vince and Shane McMahon. Their opponents were The Rock, the Undertaker, and Kane. The last wrestler left standing would be the World Champion.

Hunter wrestled The Rock during most of the match. Kane then took Hunter down with a piledriver. The Rock won the match and the title.

Hunter was no longer the WWF World Champion. But he remained one of the WWF's top wrestlers. He continued to wrestle in main-event matches throughout the world.

Chapter 5

Triple H Today

Hunter has been a wrestling fan his entire life. He likes to watch and learn from other wrestlers. He also studies tapes of great wrestlers of the past.

Hunter's interest in learning about the wrestling business led Vince McMahon to call him "the biggest student of the game." Soon, other wrestlers nicknamed Hunter "The Game." Fans also started calling him by this name.

Other Titles

On April 3, 2001, Hunter wrestled Chris Irvine for the Intercontinental Championship. Irvine

Hunter's fans call him "The Game."

At that point, it wasn't about me...it was about that match. I made the decision at that point to finish the match.
—Hunter Hearst Helmsley,
WWF.com, 5/23/01

wrestles as Chris Jericho. Hunter defeated Jericho to win his third Intercontinental title.

On April 10, Hunter lost the Intercontinental title to Jeff Hardy. He won it back six days later. He held the title until May 20. That night, he lost the title to Kane.

Hunter became a Tag Team Champion for the first time in 2001. On April 29, he teamed with Steve Austin to defeat the Undertaker and Kane for the Tag Team title.

A Serious Injury

On May 21, Hunter and Austin defended their Tag Team title against Chris Jericho and Chris Benoit. Late in the match, Austin was wrestling Jericho. Hunter came into the ring to hit Jericho from behind. Hunter planted his left leg down as he moved forward. He felt a sharp pain shoot up his leg.

Hunter's left leg no longer supported his weight. But he wanted to finish the match.

Hunter was seriously injured during a tag team match against Chris Benoit and Chris Jericho (right).

Jericho ran out of the ring. Hunter limped after him.

Hunter grabbed Jericho and put him on top of the announcer's table. He tried to do a Pedigree on Jericho. But Jericho put Hunter in the Walls of Jericho. Jericho pushed Hunter down on top of the table. He then grabbed Hunter's legs and put them underneath his arms. He turned around to twist Hunter's body.

Jericho let go of Hunter and went back into the ring to help Benoit. Hunter limped into the ring with a sledgehammer. He raised the hammer to hit Jericho. Jericho moved. Hunter hit Austin instead. Benoit pushed Hunter out of the ring as Jericho covered Austin for the pin. Hunter lay on the floor outside the ring. Two referees helped him into an ambulance outside the arena.

Doctors told Hunter he had torn the quadriceps muscle in his left thigh. On May 23, Hunter had an operation to fix the torn muscle. He spent the next eight months getting his leg back in shape.

Return to the Ring

On January 4, 2002, Hunter returned to the WWF. He teamed with Kane to defeat Chris Jericho and Kurt Angle at a show in Binghamton, New York. Three days later, he returned to WWF TV for the first time since his injury.

On January 20, Hunter competed in the Royal Rumble in Atlanta, Georgia. He defeated 29 other wrestlers to win the tournament.

On January 20, 2002, Hunter won the Royal Rumble.

Hunter continued to wrestle well. On March 17, 2002, he faced Chris Jericho at WrestleMania 18 in Toronto, Ontario. Hunter defeated Jericho to become pro wrestling's Undisputed Champion.

Outside the Ring

Hunter still lives in New Hampshire. He is close to his parents and sister. He spends time with his family when he is not traveling.

Hunter has done some acting. In 1999, he played a wrestler on an episode of *The Drew Carey Show.* He has appeared on the TV shows *Saturday Night Live, Grown Ups, Pacific Blue, MADtv*, and *The Weakest Link.* He also appears at pro wrestling events.

Hunter has said he would consider acting in movies. But his biggest interest still is the wrestling business. Hunter works with writers and officials on ideas for matches and storylines. He also gives younger wrestlers advice on their skills and careers. Hunter hopes to continue to work in pro wrestling when his wrestling career is over.

Hunter sometimes appears at events such as the Macy's Thanksgiving Day Parade in New York City.

Career Highlights

1969—Hunter is born July 27 in New Hampshire.

1992—Hunter wrestles his first professional match as Terra Ryzing.

1994—Hunter joins WCW; he soon changes his wrestling name to Jean-Paul Levesque.

1996—Hunter joins the WWF as Hunter Hearst Helmsley and later wins the WWF Intercontinental Championship.

1997—Hunter teams with Shawn Michaels and Chyna to form D-Generation X.

1999—Hunter wins two WWF World Championships.

2000—Hunter wins his third and fourth WWF World Championships.

2001—Hunter wins his third and fourth Intercontinental titles; he also teams with Steve Austin to win the WWF Tag Team Championship.

2002—Hunter returns to the ring after an injury and wins both the Royal Rumble and the Undisputed Championship.

Words to Know

bodybuilder (BOD-ee-bil-duhr)—a person who develops muscles through exercise and diet

disqualification (dis-kwahl-uh-fuh-KAY-shuhn)—a decision that prevents someone from taking part in or winning an activity; athletes can be disqualified for breaking the rules of their sport.

Pedigree (PED-uh-gree)—the name of Hunter's signature move

quadriceps (KWAH-druh-seps)—a muscle in the front part of the thigh

referee (ref-uh-REE)—a person who makes sure athletes follow the rules of a sport

signature move (SIG-nuh-chur MOOV)—the move for which a wrestler is best known; this move also is called a finishing move.

To Learn More

Alexander, Kyle. *Pro Wrestling's Most Punishing Finishing Moves.* Pro Wrestling Legends. Philadelphia: Chelsea House, 2001.

Burgan, Michael. *The Rock: Pro Wrestler Rocky Maivia.* Pro Wrestlers. Mankato, Minn.: Capstone High-Interest Books, 2002.

Hunter, Matt. *Ric Flair: The Story of the Wrestler They Call "The Nature Boy."* Pro Wrestling Legends. Philadelphia: Chelsea House, 2001.

Molzahn, Arlene Bourgeois. *Mankind: Pro Wrestler Mick Foley.* Pro Wrestlers. Mankato, Minn.: Capstone High-Interest Books, 2002.

Useful Addresses

Professional Wrestling Hall of Fame
P.O. Box 434
Latham, NY 12110

World Wrestling Entertainment, Inc.
1241 East Main Street
Stamford, CT 06902

Internet Sites

Do you want to learn more about Triple H?
Visit the FactHound at *http://www.facthound.com*

FactHound can track down many sites to help you. All
the FactHound sites are hand-selected by our editors.
FactHound will fetch the best, most accurate information
to answer your questions.

IT'S EASY! IT'S FUN!
1) Go to *http://www.facthound.com*
2) Type in: 073681311X
3) Click on "FETCH IT" and FactHound will put you on
   the trail of several helpful links.

You can also search by subject or book title. So, relax
and let our pal FactHound do the research for you!

Index

Austin, Steve, 6, 21, 27, 32, 36, 39

babyface, 8, 25
bodybuilding, 11–12

Cactus Jack, 29–30
Chyna, 7, 22, 23

D-Generation X (DX), 23–25

family, 11, 17, 40
Flair, Ric, 15
Foley, Mick, 5, 29, 30.
    See also Cactus Jack, Mankind

Hall, Scott, 19–21
heel, 8, 22, 25

injury, 24, 36–37, 39
IWF, 14

Jericho, Chris, 36–37, 39, 40

Kane, 28, 33, 36, 39
Kowalski, Walter, 12–14

Levesque, Jean-Paul, 8, 16–17, 19

Mankind, 5–8, 22–23, 27, 28, 29
McMahon, Vince, 6, 17, 21, 27, 33, 35
Michaels, Shawn, 20–21, 23, 24

Nash, Kevin, 19–21

Pedigree, 6, 8, 19, 22, 29, 30, 37

Rock, The, 22, 24–25, 28–29, 30–31, 33

Terra Ryzing, 8, 14, 16

World Championship Wrestling (WCW), 14, 15, 16–17, 21, 32
WrestleMania, 30, 40

BOSTON PUBLIC LIBRARY

3 9999 04723 966 8

EG

EGLESTON SQUARE LIBRARY
2044 Columbus Avenue
Roxbury, MA 02119